REVEALED TO HEAL:
OVERCOMING CHURCH RAPE

REVEALED TO HEAL: OVERCOMING CHURCH RAPE

AN UNVEILING TRUTH:
FINANCIAL, PHYSICAL & EMOTIONAL ABUSE WITHIN THE BODY OF CHRIST

By:
Pastor Tahira Staten-Murphy

XULON PRESS

Xulon Press
2301 Lucien Way #415
Maitland, FL 32751
407.339.4217
www.xulonpress.com

Printed in the United States of America.

ISBN-13: 978-1-6312-9423-5

TABLE OF CONTENTS

"THIS IS ME"

The Journey of Tahira Staten (Mims) Murphy and what it took to overcome!

After more than thirty years, I have finally come to the place in my life that I know, without a shadow of a doubt, what it means that if it had not been for the Lord not only being on my side but also keeping my mind when I thought I was going to lose it (multiple times) and giving me the strength to choose a "better way" instead of killing someone or having him or her killed, I would have been lost, dead, locked up, or all of the above. But through my journey, I've found hope, peace, and a greater understanding that I am more than a conqueror, and because of this, I am an overcomer. I share my story with you because you too can be an overcomer. *"For the wages of sin is death, but the gift of God is eternal life." (Rom. 6:1).*

So, choose life even when you feel death!

****

At the tender age of eight, while sitting on the second row next to my grandmother at Purity Baptist Church, I listened to the pastor preaching about salvation and the penalty for sin. As he spoke, something on the inside of me leaped, and I felt the pull of God upon my heart. As the pastor finished his message, he "opened the doors of the church" and invited those who had never openly confessed Jesus as their personal Lord and Savior to come up to the front. He said that if they believed in their heart that God raised Jesus from the dead and they wanted to be saved and become part of the body of Christ and the fellowship, they should come forward and give the pastor their hand but give God their heart. It was then, with tears streaming down my face, that I stood up, walked to the front of the church and told the pastor that I wanted to be baptized and saved.

This is when my spiritual journey began, and my life would never be the same from that day forward.

I didn't know what was in store for me after being baptized and giving my life to serve Jesus. But I remembered the stories of victory, as well as defeat, spoken by many in the church and within our family. And I knew beyond the shadow of a doubt that it was better to be with Jesus than without Him. I remembered hearing testimonies from the deacons and deaconesses of how God had made ways for them out of difficult situations. But, honestly, I still didn't understand what that all really meant.

When I was around twelve years old, I was young, full of energy, and loved the Lord, but I was also curious about what the "world" had to offer. I was not, at that time, interested in sex, drugs, or alcohol because my grandfather was a drunk, my mother was a functioning alcoholic, and my father would have people over the house to drink cognac, roll joints, and smoke cigars, all of which disgusted me. But still, curiosity about life and things to come seemed to attract me and started to pull me in.

From time to time, we would go over to my Aunt Dee's house (she had a large house and cooked the best food) to get away from the normal hustle and bustle of life. She lived on the outskirts of the city, and we lived in the inner city. But every time we went over to my aunt's house, my uncle (my aunt's husband, who was an ordained deacon in the church) would always ask me to sit on his lap, and he would hold me tight and bounce me up and down. This had been going on since I was about nine or ten, but now, I was a pre-teen, and I felt like this was out of the ordinary—strange, almost perverse. But I figured this couldn't be as bad as I thought because we were taught to be respectful and do as we were told by adults, and we wouldn't be around people who our parents didn't trust, so why not trust my uncle and do as he said.

At the age of sixteen, I moved in with my grandmother. My mother had me move in with her because I was going to a new school uptown and it was easier for me to take the bus to and from her house, rather than from my own. Also, Grandma suffered from asthma, and this was a way to make sure someone was nearby if she needed help (well, at least that was what I was told, but it didn't make a lot of sense because my Aunt Jeanette lived directly across the street from Grandma). Later, I figured out that moving in with Grandma was a way for my mom to have someone looking after me— not because I needed supervision but because my mom didn't want me in the house alone to do who knows what (oh, but I know exactly what I could have done, and it wasn't good!). See, I was blessed with a smile that could light up a room but was also very flirtatious and promiscuous. I was very attractive and athletic (with a body like the "gods," as many would say). My mom worked two and three jobs to make ends meet, since my dad was either away on military duty or just a fly-by-night and my older sister, Koya, had already gone away to college, so being with Grandma was the best place for me.

It was like a generational curse. From my earlier years, I saw and learned to, "Use what you have to get what you want." It was not the right way of life, but I didn't know otherwise.

As I lived with Grandma, she kept a tight rein on me (as best as she could). She would take me to church, teach me about God and His ways, and pray with and for me. I was saved, but I was not sanctified. I knew about Christ and believed in God's Word, but I didn't have a personal relationship with Him. I still did what I wanted to do and had no conviction within me. But even so, there was still something on the inside of me that would not allow me to go too far. I would feel out of place among friends when they did wrong. I was different.

It wasn't just Grandma who helped me during this season of my life. My Aunt Jeanette did too. She saw something in me that I didn't see in myself. We had a large family with many cousins, and she had a child of her own, yet she would pull me with her to go to church. Aunt Jeanette was part of a Holiness/Pentecostal fellowship, and it seemed like she went to church every day of the week. She was very serious about her walk with the Lord, and she would take me to church with her whenever she had an opportunity—morning, noon, and even night services.

One particular Friday night service that Aunt Jeanette took me to changed my life for the better. The people there were full of the Holy Spirit (speaking in tongues, shouting, repenting, praising and worshipping God), and I had grown to love being in such a high-spirited, powerful atmosphere. It gave me hope, life, and a sense of peace that I could overcome anything through Jesus Christ. And then it happened—the power of God hit me like a ton of bricks. It didn't take anyone to push me down on the floor, spit on me, shake me, yell, and tell me to say things that I didn't understand—the power of God fell (up)on me, and I started crying and lifting my hands. Then my Aunt Jeanette told one of the altar workers to "tarry" with me. *What's tarrying?* I thought quickly. The Spirit of God was so powerful; I couldn't stop crying. It was an amazing feeling. So, I fell to my knees, and the altar worker told me to just thank God for gifting me with

His Holy Spirit and call on the name of Jesus. I continued to thank and praise God until He was finished with me.

I don't know how, and I don't know why, but that night, I was filled with the precious gift of the Holy Spirit with the evidence of speaking in tongues. I was so full of the Holy Spirit that by the time my Aunt Jeanette took me home, I still was speaking in tongues when we got there. Hallelujah!

About six months later, still around the age of sixteen, I met my future husband, Marlin Mims, at church. We sang in the choir and were part of ministries within the church. But there were secrets that I withheld from him, dark places in my life which I didn't tell anyone about. They were dirty, painful, perverse things about my past that I was ashamed of, so I lived my life as if nothing negative had ever happened to me. I had convinced myself that the past was the past and that as long as I didn't tell anyone, those secrets and situations would go to the grave with me. I was now filled with the Holy Ghost, and I thought that my past had been totally wiped away clean. It had been, but thoughts of my past still haunted me.

After three years of dating Marlin, we were preparing for marriage, and it was then that we were asked if my cousin, Pastor Young, would officiate our wedding. I never knew that people could hide secrets so deep within themselves that they actually start to believe their own lies. This was what happened with me. I had not spoken to anyone about my cousin and the things which had happened to me while at my Grandma's house (especially after she had passed away). I never spoke about how my uncle came over to the house and had me "sit on his lap" as he held me down and placed his hand down my panties and rubbed my vagina and stomach. I never mentioned the mental torment and complex thoughts of how to deal with a pastor who was my predator. Then, unfortunately, the pain started to infiltrate inside of me. My mind became bombarded with my past, my heart started to ache like never before, and I couldn't hold it in any longer. At this point, I thought I would have a mental breakdown—not because I was facing situations that I had tried to bury for years but because I had suppressed the pain for so long that it had become a bitter root in my life. I had never dealt with it and had just pushed it under the rug, praying no one would ever move it and see all the dirt hidden underneath.

At this point, I had to reveal what had happened to me to someone, but who could I trust when the pain came from those who I'd trusted and were leaders in the church?

I decided to come clean with Marlin and reveal that which was tormenting me. I couldn't ask him to trust me if I couldn't reveal my deepest hurts and secrets. So, at the age of nineteen, I married Marlin and I was finally able to step forward with a newfound sense of relief from the guilt and shame I had carried within myself for so many years. I was able to release the pain and guilt of my past, withholding nothing. I then felt free, but I wasn't free-indeed yet.

Marlin and I continued in the faith and worked diligently to grow together with God as our Father, Jesus as our Savior, and the Holy Spirit as our guide. A few years later, I was called into ministry as the youngest deaconess (similar to a missionary) of the church. The pastor had spoken with me and Marlin and identified the "call of God" upon my life. I was a different bird. I didn't do as everyone else. I had been set apart at an early age for the work of the ministry, and I accepted the ministry elevation.

I was now around the age of twenty-one. One day, I was sitting at my desk at work, and I heard a voice say, "Release with fire!" *What? Who was that?* I thought, as I stood up and looked around. But no one was in my immediate area. So, I sat back down and kept working. Again, the words spoke, "Release with fire!" I stood up again and looked around, but nothing. So again, I sat back down. But this last time, the words came as if someone had yelled at me—with force and conviction—**"Release with fire!"** Then I jumped up out of my chair and knew that it was the voice of the Lord that I heard, loud and clear. Shaken yet amazed, I left my office and told my husband what had happened, and we went to speak with our pastor. Wisdom kicked in, and he gave me wise counsel. He said, "Pray and ask the Holy Spirit to reveal to you what God wants out of your life."

I then accepted my call into the ministry as an evangelist.

Many years later, my Uncle Bay-Boy passed, and the family choir was asked to sing at his homegoing. One of my cousins and I were asked to lead a song, and that's when we were told that our cousin, Pastor Young, would be officiating. Suddenly, I felt sick. Hold up! I thought I was delivered and free from this pain. Why was I still dealing with frustration and hurt and feeling sick to my stomach when it came to him? I realized that I had been delivered but the battle was in my mind. The thoughts, the flashbacks, the pain—all of it came back as if it was starting all over again. Then my mind went back to my uncle (Aunt Dee's husband) and how he would touch me. *This must stop **now**,* I told myself.

Now I was ordained and preaching, teaching, and evangelizing to many. I could find words of hope and encouragement for the best or least of them. I had gone to seminary school, participated in ministry trainings and courses, taught Bible studies and youth groups, held shut-ins and all night prayer services— you name it. I was involved. So why was I going through all these emotional rollercoasters? Why wasn't I able to move past my anger and rescentment towards my cousin (Pastor Young)? I realized, I really never forgave him – and I still was not "free indeed". I made a mental note about myself and prayed through the service and moved on with my life.

Months later, during Sunday service, I heard the pastor make a comment which was not biblically-based. In fact, it was almost manipulative. So, after service, I approached him, and immediately, he rebuked me and told me, "The next time you come to me about something I said, make sure you have your biblical facts first!" That challenged me, so I read and read and studied and studied and found that, yes, I was correct. Manipulation from anyone is wrong, especially coming from the pulpit. After some time, I went back to the pastor, and he recognized his wrongdoings, and we moved on.

Years later, my family and I relocated to another state. We joined a fellowship and immediately started working in the ministry. The more we participated in the ministry efforts, the more we found ourselves being segregated by fellow church-goers and cliques within the church because we didn't do things the way they did. See, we were not babes in the Lord, so we did not jump and do immediately as everyone else or when someone told us to do something. We were slow to speak, quick to listen, and slow to become angry, but that wasn't good enough for some of them.

The cliques targeted our children and started speaking ill-will of them. How could this be? Sometimes we felt the people outside the church house were more spiritual and loving than those within the church building. What's wrong with this picture? What was worse was that the pastor never stopped them, although he knew their behaviors and ways. See, they manipulated not only those within the church but would target the pastor as well. Lord, have mercy.

Not even a year or two later, the devil got into my marriage. Separation? No—divorce. We had counseled, encouraged, and helped so many. This time, we needed counsel, encouragement, and for someone to help us. How could this happen to us? We lived God's Word and shared it with others. We hid God's Word in our hearts that we might not sin against Him and had been faithful. Or had we? Was it me? Had I sinned against God? Trying to figure out what I had done perplexed my mind. My hands weren't always clean nor my heart, so I was guilty of sin, even as a leader in the church. This was one of the hardest times of my life. I was divorced yet still holding up the blood-stained banner that Jesus is able to keep you and God loves you. Now, more than ever, I had to practice everything that I was preaching. I had to be the first partaker and apply this all to myself. So, I sat myself down from doing ministry work. Why? Hurting people hurt people, and I didn't want to spread my toxic attitude, hurtful ways and feelings, and unforgiving actions upon anyone else. It was a hard lesson, but it had to take place.

During this time, I started pouring my whole heart out to the Lord, withholding nothing. Many nights, I cried and wondered, *Why me*? Then the Holy Spirit would respond, "Why not you?" There were many nights not eating and trying to cover it up by saying I was fasting when my children asked why I wasn't having any food. There were many days and nights trying to figure out my next steps.

Life was hard, but I had learned by this time to never give up on God because He surely never gave up on me. It was at this point that I was restored and renewed. God had turned my tears into gladness and given me joy for my sorrow. I then returned to full-time ministry. My pastor blessed me, and I was on a path full of hope yet again.

Then came another shift in my life. During a visit back to my home state, I met a gentleman named Lloyd. We weren't looking for any new relationship from what we told each other because we both had baggage. We were both content with being single. But God had another plan, and He knew exactly what we both needed.

As written in our vows, "One wanted to heal, while another was broken. One wanted to love, while the other wanted to be loved. Two people seeking what each other was willing to give, and because God knew the desire of both hearts, He brought together two souls at a time that neither realized they needed each other. And with a single tap on the shoulder, two different coasts collided, and their worlds, being so different, became as one. Voided places within each of them were filled, broken hearts were mended, and a love was birthed stronger than either had ever experienced. And God was gloried through the holy matrimony of these two souls."

Lloyd and I married, and I revealed my all to him. This allowed him the ability to know how to pray for and with me and for us to know how to counteract the enemy when he tried to peak his ugly head.

See, life doesn't stop after divorce, after abuse, after struggles, or after pain. With God, it can all be made new. God healed my brokenness through His Word and gave me strength and peace to love again.

Then, when I wasn't looking, God blessed me yet again. When I stopped trying to figure things out and just allowed God to be God in my life, He poured more of His unconditional love into me. I had a moment of release, and as if I was giving birth to another child, I started writing. God had given me the strength to reveal my hurt and pain to help someone who may be thinking about suicide, as I had—to help that young man who thinks his sexuality is questionable, because I did; to speak to that woman who is overprotective of their children because she wants to guard them from all the predators, because that sure enough was me; to speak to that person who feels used and abused by the church by giving more money or more time but when needed help from the church, the church couldn't or wouldn't help (my next book is called *DEADication: Killing Yourself for the Church (Balancing Your Time Between God, Family, and the Church)*; to encourage that person who wants to seek revenge but knows it's not the right thing to do. This was me too. I saw "bars," as my mother used to say. I wanted to speak to that person who struggles to make ends meet and goes back and forth on paying tithes and offering versus paying bills and keeping shelter and food for his or her family—yes, you too. I wanted to write to the person who has endured the pain and shame of abuse—sexual, emotional, financial, and even verbal—by trusted leaders, family, or friends and now doesn't know where to turn. This is for you as well.

Now, thirty years later, I still have good days and bad. Why? Because I have come to realize that, yes, God fully delivered me, but the devil wants to try and bring my past up in effort to distract me from the truth. But I am a victor and not a victim, and I am able to help others and relate to them in many ways in an effort to bring hope, assurance, and peace.

This is my story, but you have one of your own. It is not easy dealing with the quiet storms within yourself. I am now not only free from my guilt and shame, I am "free indeed," and this is available for you too.

So, now I reveal how to heal and overcome "Church Rape."

INTRODUCTION

*H*E TOUCHED ME—OH, YES, HE *just touched me. What just happened? I don't quite understand. I went to talk about my problems, so how did this whole conversation turn from helping me to now hurting me?*

I was sitting at home thinking to myself, *What did I do to bring this on, and how did I let myself get into this situation? All I was trying to do was get some help, wisdom, and understanding from the church leader. Maybe I led him on with my smile. Maybe he thought I was making a pass because I was engaging in the conversation, or maybe he saw something in me that invited him to a place that I never knew as a child could be explored.*

These, along with many thoughts, are constantly going through the minds of people within the church. Some have experienced unwanted gestures, touches, looks, comments, passes, gropes, sniggles, perverse conversations, and things which should not happen or be said among those within the body of Christ. Unfortunately, many have fallen prey to church rape or church abuse, not just physically but emotionally, financially, and even gang rape, which I refer to as clique abuse.

There can be hidden lies among leaders surrounding encounters and instances where righteousness and freedom in the faith are hard to find; nonetheless, many search and wonder if there are actually truthful and honest people within the church house and religious communities, even among our leadership.

Do I have to live daily with the quiet storm inside of me? Who can I trust when my pastor is the predator? Why do I keep dealing with the mind games of playing on words, which is causing me to experience an emotional rollercoaster as I'm being raped in my mind? Then I have the guilt trips and the schemes to get me to give all that I have financially to show my love for the preacher, which is really not for God.

The manipulation from the pulpit causes me to wonder if I'm spiritually grounded. Then I face the fact that if I'm not part of the cliques, then I must be part of the problem. So, I'm gang raped by groups of people who want to force their ways, opinions, and decisions on others for their own gain.

Why me, God? Why me? So, it's time to break the silence. It's time to unveil the truth of the lies within the body of Christ, not to bring shame or reproach upon the church but to bring freedom, faith, hope, restoration, joy, and love to all those men, women, boys, and girls who have unfortunately been victimized by church rape. The time has come to reveal it for God to heal it.

Rape, molestation, sex, manipulation, and control are very rarely discussed inside the church, let alone among the body of Christ as a whole. Church leaders find themselves skirting around these topics because they assume it will become taboo if the truth of some personal actions and cover-ups by many of those who hold titles and are looked upon in the church with high esteem are revealed. Nevertheless, it happens more often than not. People come to church—the building, that is—looking at it as a place of safety and refuge. They meet together to not only receive words of encouragement and hope but to come together as a congregation, a family of believers, and a group united for the same cause. Yet, there are times when many forget that the church "building" is a hospital for the spiritually sick.

Just because someone looks healthy and whole on the outside does not mean he or she is healthy and whole internally. But we are the church—the people, not the building. When we remember that, we will no longer blame the church but find the root of the problem and pluck it out.

CHAPTER 1

FINANCIAL RAPE

WILL A MAN ROB GOD? *Yes, he robs Him by not giving his tithes and offering ... so you are cursed with a curse. So, bring all your tithes into the storehouse that there may be meat in my house and prove me now that I would not open up the windows of heaven and pour you out a blessing that you would not have room enough to receive.* (Malachi 3:8-10)

We've heard this time and time again mentioned from the pulpit. Preachers, deacons, bishops, apostles, pastors, and even laymen have given this proclamation that if you don't tithe and give an offering, then you're cursed, and not only are you cursed, but you are cursed with a curse. But hold up—there is some truth to be revealed here. Yes, tithing and giving are parts of our obedience to God. They are prerequisites of being children of God. Giving of our time, talent, and treasure all coincide with being a Christian. Jesus gave, so we ought to give also, right? We understand that it is more blessed or beneficial to "give" then it is to receive, but many times, we never studied to show ourselves approved as workmen who do not need to be ashamed but rightly divide the Word of truth. But what does this really mean? What is Malachi 3 really saying? Am I really cursed with a curse if I don't give 10 percent of all my income? Am I doomed because I didn't have anything financially to give to the church?

What's really going on here? I want to give, and when I am able to give, I won't hesitate, but now the play on words and confusion from the leaders has me in bondage to my mind (over-thinking, perplexed, stressed, and almost paralyzed) because I believe what the preacher taught and what she said—bottom line: no money, no blessing. Give more; receive more. And if I give less than 10 percent of all my income, I'm robbing God and the church. Then you tell me that I must not trust God because I paid my rent and purchased food for my children and I didn't bring the money to church first. Would God curse me for taking care of my responsibilities He blessed me with first? Isn't that called being a good steward?

So realistically, I'm screwed against my will because I must buy my blessings; otherwise, I'm cursed. But we have been taught that obedience is better than sacrifice (1 Samuel 15:22-24). But who are we obeying? God or man? Scripture teaches us that we are supposed to follow "them" (those who lead us and teach us according to the Word of God) as they follow Christ (1 Corinthians 11:1), but what happens when they stop following Christ and start following after their own fleshly desire?

Financial abuse and manipulation are real, and they are wrong. God never intended it to be this way. He set the bar, the standard, the order regarding proper giving starting with the priest, the pastor, and the ministry under-shepherds. But many leaders in the church have twisted it to forcefully make you give financially even when it hurts and all you want is for the bleeding and pain to stop. The penetration of the words, "If you don't tithe and give an offering, then you are cursed," playing over and over again is both a mental and financial abuse, and it is overwhelming. It's one thing to encourage and teach the people to become faithful givers; yet, it is another thing to manipulate and discourage the people through threats and scare-tactics to give without understanding. "In all thy getting, get understanding (Proverbs 4:7)." The time has come to reveal to heal and put an end to financial rape!

Financial Rape: Tithes & Offerings

After taking three buses, I finally made it to church—late, but I'm here.

Then from the pulpit, I hear, "It's offering time, and if you came to church without something to give, the Bible says you're cursed with a curse because you're robbing God!" People around me start cheering and clapping, reaching for envelopes and checkbooks. Excitement feels the air, and it starts to feel like all eyes are on me to see why I am not pulling out any money. Sitting in the pew watching the offering basket go from person to person, aisle after aisle, my palms start to sweat, and my heart starts to race because I want to give but I can't.

I start reaching into my purse hoping that maybe there is something there that I can give. A dollar. A penny. Something. Anything. But I realize that I used all the money I had to get on the bus to make it to church. And then it starts happening again—the guilt sits in, and I wonder if my struggles are because I'm not giving to God as the pastor has taught. Is my struggle because I chose to feed my children first and I had nothing left to put in the basket? Is my struggle because I didn't give of the first fruit of my increase to the church, yet knowing that if I gave the 10 percent of my check to the church off the top (before paying anyone or anything else), if I had to go back and ask the church to help me, they would deny me?

Yes, I know this feeling all too well. It is now becoming my new normal. I come to church to hear and receive the Word of God, but I'm stressed coming in, stressed while here, and then stressed leaving. No one in the church has explained to me how to balance my finances. I grew up in a home where we never discussed finances or having good credit. We were taught to go to church. Pay your tithes. Go to work and go home. Anything outside of that was sin.

But now, I'm stuck between a rock and a hard place. I hear the testimonies of many saying that because they tithed, God has blessed them. But will God stop blessing me because I don't have anything to give? What if I didn't have a job? Would God not help me?

So, I went and asked my pastor what to do, and he said, "Daughter, if you don't give, you will be worse off. For you can't afford not to tithe and give an offering." Oh no, I don't need worse. My hands are tied, my heart starts pounding, and I'm sitting in church full of anxiety. So, after service, I go back to the pastor and ask again, "Is there anything I can do to meet the needs of my home and pay my tithes when I don't have enough to do both?" He looks at me and places his hand on my shoulder and says, "If you love me, you will trust what I tell you. God will help you only if you bring all your tithes to the storehouse. If you take care of the church first, God will then take care of you." I am abused and manipulated in my mind by the thoughts penetrating me about my finances and the church.

Financial Rape: Give Until It Hurts

I've given so much over the years until it hurts. I freely gave all that I had to support the ministry financially, but life turned for me, and I looked at church from a different perspective the day I found out that my check was short and I didn't have enough to pay my bills and tithes, let alone give an offering. So, I prayed and asked God to supply my needs according to His riches in glory through Christ Jesus. I declared and recited in faith all that I knew and read from the Bible.

For I was what people called a faithful tither (a faithful giver). Yet my bills still needed to be paid, and I was stuck at a cross-road. "Give in faith" continued to run across my mind. "If you don't pay all your tithes, you are a thief and robbing God," was etched through my brain.

Do I give my normal 10 percent although my check is short or pay my bills? And then it hit me like a ton of bricks. The pastor taught us that if we don't give, we curse ourselves. So, I went to one of the church leaders and asked what to do. "How do I choose? I trust God, and I know what we have been taught from the pulpit."

Then the answer came from the mouth of the church leader. "How do you say you trust God if you don't bring all your tithes into the storehouse first? Your 'first fruit' is what is required. Apparently, you don't trust or love God."

I was crushed. Yes, I love and trust God with all my heart. I didn't want to lean on my own understanding. I needed direction. I needed clarity. So, I gave. And gave. And gave, not missing a beat. No matter how much it hurt me and my family, I gave my 10 percent because I believed I was doing what God said and I followed the teachings by my pastor.

But one day, I got home from Bible study, and on my table was an eviction notice. I froze in place and said, "God, You promised to supply all my needs according to Your riches in glory. You told me obedience was better than sacrifice, and I have given my tithes and offering faithfully unto you." So the next day, I went back to the church and asked for help, and they told me they would check the records to see how much I had given over the years.

After they checked the records and clearly saw that I was one of the church's top givers, they responded that they could only give me 10 percent of what I had given to the church over the years. But that still wasn't enough to cover the lack which I had and the eviction which I was facing. There was no food in our refrigerator, and rent was due, and all the church could tell me at that point was that God would help me and they would pray for me. And the inevitable happened—we were evicted from our home.

What just happened here? If I didn't give, I was cursed. And now that I have been giving faithfully, I'm still cursed. Cursed with a curse. Something's wrong with this picture.

<u>Financial Rape: Fellowship vs. Social Club</u>

Sitting at home minding my own business, I started sorting through the mail and saw a letter from our church. Anxiously wondering why there was a letter from the church, it was addressed to my husband, so I didn't open it. I waited until he came home for him to open it. Curiosity was knocking at my heart. I was hoping that they were sending a letter to check on us because we had not been there in a while. Life had been challenging, and most of the time, we barely had enough money to make ends meet, so we stayed at home, praying and worshipping God together because we didn't have enough to put gas in the car to drive to church or work. Over a year had passed, and no one from the church had called to check on us, but we still believed in our hearts that we were members and that they cared. Why? Because we are a family of believers. So, I stood on that fact. Finally, my husband arrived and before he could get his coat off, I asked him to open the letter, and inside it said:

"Praise the Lord, Brother. We sadly regret to inform you that due to your lack of financial support to this ministry, we have taken your name off the church roster, effective immediately.

You are no longer a member of this church. We will keep you in our prayers. God Bless."

As my eyes glanced through the words, my heart started to pound, and I looked at my husband, who was still a baby in the Lord. He had just recently given his life to serve Jesus a little over a year ago and was baptized at this church, yet no one had called to check on us this past year to see if we were alive or dead. However, because he had not given financially over a period of time, he was dropped from the church membership. What kind of foolishness was this?

We didn't know that being a member of the church and part of the fellowship of believers was predicated upon how much money we gave to the church. It didn't state he was dropped because he was not attending. All they cared about was the money—not the spirit or the soul. What happened to the body being fitly joined together and every joint supplying? What happened to fellowshipping one with another and that the stronger should bear the infirmities of the weaker? What happened to you needing me and I needing you?

My husband was crushed. He felt abused and mistreated, and he didn't understand how his finances, or the lack thereof, would stop him from fellowshipping with the so-called saints of God. So, I had to go further. I had to dig deeper. My husband felt violated, like someone had forced themselves and their decision on him without permission.

I called the church and spoke with the trustee. She explained that since I had paid money to the church, I was able to continue as part of the membership but if no one contributes, they are dropped. But wait a minute. Was this a church or a social club? After that conversation, we both felt like we were part of a civil association, not a body of believers, not the church. Yes, it takes money to advance the kingdom of God. Yes, it takes money to keep the building running and functioning. But you forced your actions on me and my family without consent, without speaking and talking it out. You did as you pleased and dared us to think or say otherwise.

Financial Rape: Where Does My Money Go?

I sit and watch as people run to the altar, not for prayer or repenting from their sinful ways, not even coming for salvation, but running and dropping money at every word the preacher speaks. I wonder if they are doing this for show or if they are doing this because they really have the money to give. But who am I to judge for the Bible tells us, "Judge not lest ye be judged with the same judgments (Matthew 7:1-2)." But what's interesting to see is that every Sunday, the same ones are running and placing money at the feet of the preacher, yet when there's someone who has a serious need, they turn their faces and their backs and walk away as if they have nothing to share.

But the Bible says, "What you've done to the least of these you've done it unto God. When I was naked you gave me clothes when I was hungry you gave me food and I was thirsty you gave me something to drink (Matthew 25:35-40)," but the church, the leaders, those with the titles, will stand in front of the church and raise money for building funds to expand the seats instead of using the money to expand outreach to others who may not be able to come to the building yet still need support.

Where does the money go after we all give? I wondered and questioned because people in need even within the congregation were being turned down for help from the church officials. So, I asked to see the financial books of the church. This was a nonprofit organization, right? But I was pushed away and told it was private information.

So, I asked to see my personal record of giving, and again, I was turned down and told, "You will get a statement at the end of the year." Now perplexed in my mind, I didn't want to think that the church was misusing the finances, but it's hard when the pastor drives a Jaguar and the first lady sports her minks. Is it me or doesn't the Bible teach that we are **all** a royal priesthood and a chosen generation (1 Peter 2:9)?

So, does that mean I wear the rags and the leaders wear the priestly robes? Regardless, am I not to question where the money goes? It was time to renew my mind because the thoughts of financial abuse were captivating it. Anger rests in the belly of a fool, so I needed to change my stinky thinking. As scriptures continued to flood my mind, I was reminded that, "As a man thinks, so is he (Proverbs 23:7) and I was now full of bad thoughts. I was not a bad person, though, so I needed to change my thinking and trust in God. I should not worry about where the money goes. Just give, right? Yes. The revealed truth was for me to trust God and just give what I have purposed in my heart and let God handle the rest.

OVERCOMING FINANCIAL RAPE

Sadly, these are classic examples of how many churches use financial gain as the measuring stick for who stays or who goes. These accounts and many others show how some people within the church will be quick to judge or misuse the Word of God to manipulate others to give—even as far as to give financially from out of what they don't have—but they never teach on how to be a faithful servant. They only teach on the importance of giving financially and what may happen if you don't. They don't teach on how to have good credit and to not live above your means. Many teach on, "If you love me, you'll give to me, and if you don't give; you're cursed. If you don't give, you can't participate in some of the other church events and affairs that some of the bigger givers participate in."

Financial manipulation and rape separate us by how much money we bring to the table. Are we buying a blessing? Are we buying a position in the church house? God forbid! Is God looking for how much we bring to the table financially, or is He looking at how much we bring to the table with the contents of our heart toward Him?

But the truth comes full circle that the curse comes when the priest doesn't give 10 percent of that which he gets from the church. See the truth in Malachi 3 teaches that the church is supposed to take care of the affairs of the preacher, the pastor, the bishop, to give them a place and time to spend focusing 100 percent on studying and preparing the Word of God for the people of God. It is from the amounts which the priest receives as income from those who give that Scripture teaches the priest is supposed to take out 10 percent of what he is given and put it back into the church. In addition, the Bible teaches that 10 percent is a baseline, a foundation, because if you use any part of the tithe according to Scripture, we are to add an additional 5 percent to our giving (Lev. 27:31 KJV). Also, the Word of God teaches us that by the blood of Jesus and His redemptive work on the Cross, we have been redeemed from the curse of the law (Galatians 3:13) and since we are no longer under the law but under grace, we are not subject to the curse which is mentioned in Old Testiment.

These are never discussed. Instead, words are twisted and manipulated to make people feel obligated to man, when honestly, our true obligation should only be to God. See, the financial giving is to supply need not greed, but if the priest is robbing God by not obeying that which is instructed, how can the pastor expect for the people under him/her to not do the same? The Bible is clear on our instructions—we ought to give and it shall be given unto you good measure pressed down shaken together running over shall men pour into our bosoms (Luke 6:38-40).

What can I do? Who do I turn to for answers? I read the Bible and get confused because it says one thing, but my pastor is teaching it another way. How do I stop this financial rape from continuously happening?

The answer is simple: "Give, and it shall be given unto you. Good measure pressed down shaken together, runneth over, shall men pour into your bosom (Luke 6:38-40)."But here is the unveiled and revealed truth. "In the measure that you give it shall be given back." Give sparingly; reap sparingly. Give bountifully; reap bountifully. So, give according to your heart. Give what God has allowed for you to sow. The woman with the two mites or coins gave more not because of the amount but because of her heart. The rich tend to give less, and the poor tend to give more. Why is that? Are you giving in hopes that your investment will profit you a bountiful return? Check your motives.

Financial Giving Starts from the Heart, Not the Pocket

Here are the keys to unlock the door and be free from the pain of financial rape or abuse:

To stop the bleeding but remain obedient to God:

(1) Search your heart first. Pray and ask God what is acceptable to give Him (an amount of money, talent, and time).

We will discuss being free from the manipulation and the unhealthy amounts of your time spent at church (the building or events and services/functions) and the importance of balance in my book _DEADication: Killing Yourself for the Church (Balancing Your Time Between God, Family, and the Church)_, and then:

(2) Freely give. Some can give more than 10 percent, and some can only give less. But the answer is to freely

give from your heart—not forcefully or grudgingly but because you want to and are not made to. The baseline is 10 percent, but many have to learn how to properly give unto the Lord and grow to give that amount consistently.

It's that simple. Come with your heart settled and your mind clear on what you plan to give based off what God has placed on your heart. And just do it—Give.

This is how some deal with financial conflictions and contradictions in the church. Although it is hard to give when the leaders seem to be soaking up the gain, the answers stand true. Just give and let God handle the rest.

This, along with many other accounts, unfortunately happens often in churches today. The pastor is placed on a pedestal, and the people or members idolize the pastor, priest, bishop, etc. in such a way that the pastor or the leader uses that control over the people to persuade them to give more financially. Greed peaks its head. This happens amongst many of the churches where members feel obligated to give because they have placed their leader in such a high position that they don't even seek God on what they should be giving and what time or season they ought to give—for the Bible teaches that there's a time and a season for everything. Also, it shows us that there are certain soils, grounds, and types of seeds that should be sown at certain times in our lives (giving of our time, talent, and/or treasure), yet we find ourselves held down and pressured to give just because "Pastor" said it, or else we will be looked upon with shame and as an unfaithful member.

CHAPTER 2

PHYSICAL RAPE

*B*ECAUSE OF THE LUST OF *the flesh, lust of the eyes, and the pride of life (I John 2:16), Jacob's daughter, Dinah, endured the shame and pain of being raped by Hamor's son, Shechem. Back then, women didn't have a right to defend or speak up for themselves for they were considered to be "property." It was bad enough that this rape occurred, but that wasn't enough for the predator.*

Shechem's father went to Jacob, not to ask him for forgiveness for what his son had done to Dinah, nor did Hamor reprimand his son for such a horrendous act. Yet Hamor went to Jacob to work out an arrangement so that his son Shechem (the "predator") would be allowed to marry the one who he had defiled (raped).

Shechem was the "chieftain"—one who was the leader, one of authority and power—yet he abused his authority by taking something that did not belong to him and then tried to possess it by demanding to his father, "Get me this girl for my wife." (Gen. 34:1-4)

What is this? This is what happened years ago in biblical times, yet some people think we are still in those times or living under those same laws. The answer is no, not so. We are no longer under the law; we are now under grace.

And because of God's grace, which is sufficient for us, we all have a voice. We have a say in every matter of our lives, and if we say "No," that is exactly what it means—"No." For the Word of God says, "Let your yes be yes, and your no be no (Matthew 5:37)."

In this day and age, unfortunately, rape, molestation, fondling, and other unwanted gestures are freely given, even when we don't want to freely receive them. Nevertheless, these things should not be named among those within the body of Christ. Why? Because any kind of action forced upon someone without consent or mutual agreement is called rape and/or abuse. And God gives us all the freedom of choice. We must choose to do that which is right or settle and condemn ourselves because of our choice to do wrong. The bottom line is, God gives us a choice.

However, we see that there are still people within the Christian communities who have neglected to choose the right path, and it has resulted in many people (men, women, boys, and girls) hurt by the careless acts of others by the use of sinful ways. Your body is the temple of the Holy Spirit, and how it is handled is a sacred thing. Many people don't look at it from that perspective. They look at the body as a tool, a gift, a treasure (which it is, but the gift and treasure are from God for His use). And when people misplace the proper functionality of a person's body, they no longer respect that which God created for His good pleasure, and perverse actions sometime occurs.

But there is grace, which is unmerited favor from God. We are privileged to know that God grants us grace so that we can move from places of despair and hurt to the places of abundance, peace, joy and love. It's time to take back your life. Don't allow for the enemy to try and trick you into settling for the harm which may have been done. Yes, many have fallen prey to the traps of the enemy, but no more. We have uncovered the lies and exposed the truth. No more church rape. No more sexual perversion and sin within the body of Christ. Today is your day of redemption!

Physical Rape: Every Rumor Isn't False–"The Warning Signs"

My world had just turned upside down. The matriarch of our family had just passed away. Grandma had paved the way for all of us and was the one who had kept the family together. I had been living with her because it was easier for me to get back and forth to school from her house and also, I would help her because oftentimes she would have asthma attacks and we did not want her to be alone. But now she was gone. This last asthma attack was her last and, unfortunately, I had not been at home to help her. But she had spoken so much into my life from birth and had always urged me to follow the path of God and to remember that family was special, especially the ones who were following the divine call of God.

She was so proud of my cousin who had gone from being a deacon to stepping into the ministry call and then finally starting his own church as a pastor. Grandma would always talk about how our family was built on faith and that through all the adversities, it was God who kept us. Many of our family members were musicians in the church, having a family choir, and some even went as far as holding positions in the church, and this all brought great joy and happiness to Grandma. But he stood out from the rest. She would talk to me about the call of God on his life and would tell me how she would have been part of his ministry if she wasn't so dedicated to her home church and that she would try and visit from time to time. But God called her home to rest before she was able to accomplish these goals.

After her death, I remained at her house alone with the family dog, and many times, my cousin (the pastor) would stop by to check on me. This was not uncommon because my mother, other family members, and friends would stop by also to ensure I was okay. Yet I still felt alone in Grandma's house and was vulnerable because I believed that it was my fault that she had died because I had not been there to help her. The inner torment and battles in my mind occupied my time. But this particular day was different. My cousin came by to check on me, and as he talked, he glanced up and down at me in a way that was uncomfortable. It was not a normal greeting but a glare, a stare. It was the look that a man gives a woman when he is attracted to her, when a boy looks at a girl and visualizes what's behind her clothes, lusting. It was that look that I had seen often by many others, but I ignored it and brushed it off because I didn't think this could be what I thought it was. So, I discredited what had just happened because there was no way he was sexualizing me with his eyes. I dismissed it and moved on.

Now, weeks had passed, and things were going good, but all of a sudden I was home alone again and he stopped by (the devil was busy). As he walked up to the door, my mind remembered the stories being said about him lately. There were rumors that he had been cheating on his wife and having affairs with women in the church, but I was hoping that they all were lies because he was a "man of the cloth," a man who led a congregation of people for God, and I never thought in a million years that he would even do such a thing. So, he stood at the door waiting for me to open it. As normal, I opened the door without reservation, giving him a hug and greeting him to make sure that everything was okay.

But it was then that he held on and was not letting me go. Then, while closing the door behind him, he started pushing me to the wall as he felt my body up and down, impressing his erect penis against my body, moving it up and down. Then he spoke words of how he wanted to enter inside of me. I pleaded with him to just stop and that this was not right. Suddenly, he stuck his tongue in my mouth to shut me up, and I pushed him off. Now seeing that I was visibly shaken at what had just happened, he decided to stop.

I didn't understand what I'd done to welcome this upon me as he smiled and said that he loved me. For these weren't words of godly love, not agape nor family love but something totally perverse. How could this happen? How could this be? This was the one who our family was so proud of, and Grandma would turn over in her grave if she knew what had just happened. But who would believe me because I was not a virgin, and many of my family members already thought that I was a harlot, a whore, loose, and out of control. But behind the scenes, they did not know the torment in my mind— that I was fighting off rape, molestation, gropes, and perverse actions that had happened to me not only this time but times before.

I had experienced rape of my mind and had been torn in my spirit by a "man of God." How could I overcome this? Who could I tell when the predator was not only a pastor but part of my family?

So this caused me to look at myself. I had thoughts that I was the reason this had happened and convinced myself that I was guilty of allowing him in the house when I was alone. I kept remembering the lesson from Grandma, "Never assume anything, and you are a young lady, so never put yourself in situations when you are alone with a man—no matter what." And then she would say, "Whenever you are unsure of what to do, stop and pray, and don't be quick to do anything because being anxious may lead to destruction."

That was it! I hadn't prayed! I told myself this over and over again. This all happened because I hadn't heeded the advice and warnings from Grandma. I had let a man, regardless of the fact that he was family, in the house alone with me. I quickly opened the door, and I let the enemy in, unknowingly.

But just at that moment, something clicked inside me. It was that love that Grandma had talked about—the love of Christ that is shed abroad in our hearts. And instead of hating my cousin, I

REVEALED TO HEAL: OVERCOMING CHURCH RAPE

started praying for him. It was that love that only Jesus can give that soothes a worried heart and a broken spirit. And suddenly, I felt sad for him. I felt bad for his wife and for his children. If he did this to me, it must be true that he was doing ungodly things to others. I kept thinking that his soul was at stake because of his actions and choices. But I wasn't a saint either. And yet, there still was the scared and broken young girl who now questioned how God could allow this to happen. But instead of turning from God, I ran to God, chasing Him and His perfect will for my life. Curiosity about the truth of God and how it was all supposed to line up in my life started boiling up in my heart with a hunger and thirst for righteousness, and my life changed for the better. My personal relationship with the Almighty One took root in my heart that day, and the healing began.

As life went on, I met a young man at church, and we started dating. Three years later, we were planning our wedding, and someone asked if I was going to let my cousin marry us. See, at this time, my cousin had become very well known in the Christian community. He had a large congregation and a serious following of people who respected and loved him.

But when his name was mentioned, thoughts of the past resurrected and started to overtake my mind. Thoughts of the pain and hurt and disrespect flowed through my being, and instead of being hurt, I became mad—mad as hell because he had never apologized. He had never thought anything of his actions and thought he had gotten away with it. But God reminded me through His Word that one day, my cousin will have to give an account for his actions and every idle word—maybe not to me but to the Almighty One—"For vengeance is mine declared the Lord (Romans 12:17-19)," and He will repay.

So, my fiancé, in his gentle way, looked at me and asked what was wrong, and I lied and said, "Nothing." But he knew me, and instead of trying to force me to talk, he allowed me time to gather my thoughts. He patiently waited until the appropriate time came, then I sat down with tears streaming down my eyes and explained to him what had happened to me when I was younger. It was then that I started to feel the ice melt away from my heart that I had been unaware was there. True forgiveness started to pour out of my soul for all the wrong that had been done to me, not only by him but by all the other predators throughout my life. I was able to be vulnerable to my fiancé and explained to him about not only this cousin but also my uncle who had fondled me when I was younger. It was then that I requested to speak with our pastor to gain wise counsel. It took me revealing it for God to heal it. I had to come to grips with the pain that I was suppressing—the anger, the frustration, the unforgiveness, and even the hatred toward all of those men who had not thought about me and were only concerned with pleasing themselves. But God showed himself strong, and the more I prayed to Him about my true feelings, the more He removed the callus from my heart, and instead of having a heart of stone, God gave me a heart of flesh. The more I prayed, the more I started to believe, and the more I believed in God and His Word, the stronger I became, and I was able to openly confess my pain and disappointments to be free indeed. "For whom the Son sets free is free indeed (John 8:36)," according to the Word of God.

Physical Rape: When My Pastor is the Predator

It was my time to meet with the pastor to discuss some questions which continuously caused me to be perplexed and confused. My appointment was his last meeting that Friday afternoon to accommodate my school schedule. When I arrived, the pastor was the only one there. I didn't think anything of it because he was my pastor. I had no reason not to trust him because he loved me as one of his sheep and was the one who was looking after my soul.

So, he asked me to wait and have a seat in his office and he would be right back. About five minutes later, he came into the office and closed the door. As he proceeded to lock it, I asked him if everything okay, and he looked into my eyes and said, "Of course, everything is okay. Why wouldn't it be?" But something inside of me was unsettled; yet I ignored it and moved on.

He asked me what was on my mind, and I began to talk. As we talked, there were times when the conversation would shift and he would say something funny and I would laugh or he would tap my knee with his hand to reassure me that everything would be okay when the conversation became a little emotionally intense.

About roughly twenty minutes into our conversation, he started moving a little closer beside me. At this point, I instantly felt as if he was getting a little too comfortable, but I was young (in my teens) and not really sure of what my mind was trying to warn me about. Then the conversation took a turn, and he started talking about how attractive I was. He started to touch my hair and gaze into my eyes and expressed how I would be an awesome catch for whatever man claimed me as his wife. So, my mind started wondering, *What the heck is happening here?* I was not sure of what in the world was getting ready to happen or why he was telling me this.

I had come there to ask questions about my life and things that pertained to the Word of God, and now, the conversation was about my physical state, how attractive I was, and how I would be a good catch for a man. So, I slid over to give some space between the two of us, and he slid a little closer toward me. I asked him again if he was okay because I didn't know what to say at this point, and he replied, "I'm fine, but I could be better if I had you."

At that point, I tried to get up to leave, and he asked, "Why are you in a rush? We are just talking. There's no reason to fear because God does not give you the spirit of fear but of power, love, and a sound mind. I'm not going to hurt you because this is something I know you have already experienced." And at that point, I screamed for help, but he said, "No one is here but us."

Then I said, "But God is here, and whatever happens, you will pay." Unfortunately, his power and strength overtook mine, and my innocence and purity were taken, and my heart was crushed.

What just happened? How could this happen? Did I invite this upon myself? Was I too engaging in the conversation? Did I smile too hard?

Physical Rape: Those Lurking in the Darkness

As a young person, going to church was exciting. We would have youth council meetings and young adult sleepovers, also called shut-ins. Many times during these shut-ins, the curiosity of "who liked who" (as far as girlfriend/boyfriend) within the church youth groups were on the minds of many of us curious, hormone-raged teenagers.

At one of the church shut-ins, there were about thirty of us all gathered together, and it was time to get ready to go to sleep. A few hours later, the youth leaders had fallen asleep, and a few of us were still wide awake. I got up to go use the bathroom, which was a little far from where we were sleeping in the church. I tiptoed from the sleeping area because I did not want to wake anyone. I looked around and noticed everyone seemed to now be sleep and I was the only one awake. Once I finished using the bathroom, I came out and was welcomed by three of the boys in the church. I didn't think anything other than that they needed to use the bathroom as well. *But why didn't they go to the men's restroom, which is located on the other side of the church?* pondered through my mind.

I started to walk away and told them they needed to go back to sleep as well. But suddenly, one of them grabbed my arm and told me that they knew that I had a crush on him. I denied it, although realistically I did, but I didn't want him to know. However, there was something inside of him that gave him the assurance that indeed I did like him, and although I said no, he took it as a yes.

Anyway, as I continued to try to walk away, he yanked my arm harder, and I told him that he was hurting me. Suddenly, the three of them pushed me back into the women's bathroom and told me if I said a word that they would not only beat me up but would find me and torment me and always find a way to hurt me more.

So I was confused, not sure of what to do. Should I scream? Should I fight? There were three of them, and everyone else was asleep. What should I do? I was not sexually active and did not know what was getting ready to take place, but I knew it wasn't good, and it wasn't what I wanted.

So, they held me down on the ground, and one of them started feeling on my body. I began to squirm violently, trying to wrestle to get loose. Then they started laughing as another put his hand down my panties and commenced to feel my vagina. At this time, the tears started to flow from my eyes as I pleaded for them to stop. I told them I wouldn't tell if they would just stop. And one kept saying, "Keep talking, and you will really know what pain is." So, I kept quiet out of fear.

Then all of a sudden, the one who I thought I liked stuck his finger inside of me. It hurt so bad. He stated, "Oh, you are so tight—you must be a virgin." I started to scream and cry, and he said, "I guess you want more pain."

Furiously, I shook my head and said, "No! Please, no!" But he didn't listen. He then pulled his night pants down and pulled mine all the way down to expose my legs.

As his friends held my body down and he covered my mouth, he entered his erect penis inside me. The pain was unbearable. I did not know what to do as he continued to thrust in and out. The pain continued to increase, and then all of a sudden, the pain turned into something totally different. I couldn't cry because it was a feeling I could not explain. My legs started to tremble, and all at once, the pain turned to unknown and unwanted pleasure. I had experienced an orgasm.

Not even knowing what had just happened, I was too exhausted to even fight. In what seemed to be forever, though only a matter of minutes, my purity had been taken, and my body had responded as if it had wanted it and enjoyed it.

The boy lying on top me smiled and said, "Looks like you enjoyed every moment. Now you better not tell anyone. I will always be your first, and you will never forget me."

Now I was totally confused because it all had happened inside of the church walls and no one was aware but me and these three guys. It wasn't the church's fault. I figured everyone who came to church loved God and respected His house. But what should I do? Who should I tell? So, I got up and saw blood on my clothes and on the floor. I cleaned it up and myself, and as I walked back to the sleeping area with tears filling my eyes, I woke up one of the counselors and told her that I got my period. She asked me if I was okay because she could tell something seemed strange, but I shook my head and said, "Everything will be fine. I'm just embarrassed. Can someone take me home?" As I arrived home, I vowed to keep this horrid ordeal to myself because I didn't want any more pain.

Years later, I was in a relationship with a young man from college, and it was getting serious. This was the time in my life when I thought I was ready to give myself to the one who I loved, but my past, which I thought I had pushed under the rug, started to reveal itself. As I sat on the couch beside my boyfriend, he and I started to kiss, and he began to caress my body. Once he started to feel toward my vagina, I became petrified and started to cry, and he stopped and asked, "What's wrong?" He said he did not want to do anything to hurt me and that if I was not ready, it was okay.

It was these comforting words that allowed me to expose to him the pain of my past, and instead of him condemning me or judging me, he stopped and prayed with me and asked God to bring healing to my mind, my body, my spirit, and my soul. These words, as he prayed, allowed for the cleansing love of Jesus to wash away years of hurt and pain and unforgiveness. But he went further and encouraged me to seek counsel—not just any counsel but godly counsel.

So, we went to go to the school chaplain together and explained what was going on, and she was able to direct me to get some help. It was the best advice anyone could have ever given me.

Now I am grown. And guess what? I married that young man. He showed me that getting godly, wise counsel is necessary to help when dealing with all situations, no matter how bad or good. He showed me godly love when I exposed my past hurt. He didn't take me at a vulnerable state and abuse it. He loved God inside me.

Also, I was able to save myself (not have any sex) until after we were married. See, in my eyes, I was still a virgin, although my virginity had been taken at a young age. Sex is a beautiful thing in the context of how God created it.

Physical Rape: I'm Not Gay

There were not many of us in church, but my mother still made me go. Her words still stick inside my head, "As for me and my whole house, we will serve the Lord. So, when I leave to go to church, everyone in my house will go with me...or else."

So, it was our normal to go every Sunday. There were times when we would go during the week for Bible study, but not all the time. But this particular Wednesday, my mom told me that we were going to church for Bible study. So, I got cleaned up and decided to actually put on some nicer clothes. We were going to the house of God, and I grew up understanding the purpose and the respect which is due to the temple where we gathered for service.

As we all dispersed into our different rooms separated by ages and/or gender, those in my age group all went into the room with a teacher and sat patiently, waiting for our Bible study class to commence. As it began, our teacher started talking to us about God's plans for men and women, the purpose of marriage, and how we ought to prepare for it when we reached a certain level in our lives. Now, at the age of thirteen, we were dealing with our hormones, puberty (for the late bloomers), pimples, peer issues, and all other sorts of drama, and now this—"marriage." As our teacher continued to talk, many of us giggled and laughed at what was being said, not because we thought it was funny but because it was an embarrassing subject, and most of us didn't know much about sex, marriage, dating, or anything else, other than what we saw on the television or overheard our parents talking about during "adult conversations."

After class ended, our teacher asked if anyone had any questions, and no one spoke up. However, I had a question and felt like this was the safest place to ask. So, I raised my hand and asked, "How do you know the time is right to become intimate or have sex with someone?" It became deafly silent in the room as if everyone had wanted to ask that same question and eagerly anticipated the answer. So the teacher, looking around at all the gazing eyes staring at her, stood to her feet and said, "You will know because your heart and your body will tell you."

My body will tell me—what does that mean? I thought. So, everyone left, but that wasn't a good enough answer for me. So, I waited for everyone to leave, and I went to the teacher and asked if that answer could be elaborated on because "my body would tell me" didn't make sense to me. Then my teacher walked past, locked the door, and came face-to-face to me. She was so close that I could feel her breath on my face. So, I took a step back, and she followed up with stepping forward. At this point, I figured I was in trouble for asking my question, so I said, "I am so sorry if I disrespected you by asking my questions or if I placed you in an awkward position during class."

My teacher replied, "No, not at all. I figured you wanted to know what it felt like to have your 'body' tell you when it is time to be intimate."

I started looking around because at this time, I was totally puzzled as to what she was talking about. Then, the unthinkable happened. She grabbed me in an embrace and started to rub her hand up and down across my breast and then quickly down to my private area.

I pushed her back with great force, and she said, "I've been watching you, and your eyes have been wandering, looking at the other girls, and I know—I understand. It is okay to be gay. I am bisexual, so I can help you to know what it feels like to be with either a man or a woman. The choice is yours." I abruptly ran out of that classroom and told my mother I would never go there again.

The entire way home, my mother kept asking me what had happened. I told her that I would go to Sunday service with her but I would never go to Bible study again. Day in and day out, my mother would question me. She even called up to the church to see if someone had seen anything or heard anything because from that day forward, I was different.

My mind was tormented by the words, "It is okay to be gay." But I was not gay. I never had a desire to be so-called "gay," but those words played in my mind. The thoughts of why she would say that tried to produce fruit (bad fruit) within me. Instead, I became a whore. I started having sex with as many men that I could. I started doing everything I could to try and get my mind off of the fact that someone who I'd respected thought that I was gay.

Physical rape isn't always mere penetration. The Bible says, "As a man thinks, so is he (Proverbs 23:7)."I felt like my woman-hood was taken from me that day. My body never felt the same. Replaying in my mind over and over, I could even remember how it felt when she rubbed my body. It was the first time anyone had caressed those areas in a sexual manner, and the bad part was, it wasn't a man who had done it.

By the age of thirty, I had used and abused many men and had mistreated them for my own gratification. All of this was just to try and prove a point to myself. But I realized that all of the damage that was done by me stemmed from the damage done to me when I was young. It took for me to stop and acknowledge my wrongdoings and to find the root of the problem. I could not use what happened to me as a reason or excuse for why I did such horrible things to others. Instead of stopping the pain, I continued it. I didn't turn to God; I turned to men. I had been just as wrong as that teacher. "Two wrongs don't make a right" is what I had learned over the years, yet I had never applied it to my own life. Forgiveness is what was needed. I had to forgive the wrong that had been done to me by my teacher and pray for her. I also needed to forgive myself for holding on to this hurt and keeping myself as a victim. But lastly, I needed to go and apologize to all of those I'd hurt along the way. They meant good, but I had an ulterior motive, and they never knew it. I am a woman, made in the image of God. I am fearfully and wonderfully made, and nobody has the right to try and speak lies into my life. But the lesson here is, I don't have to receive what people may speak for I know the truth, and the truth shall set me free. "For whom the Son sets free is free indeed (John 8:36)." And I am free from the bondage of sin and shame. I am not gay!

Physical Rape: My First Lady Wants Me as Her First Lady

I was raised to honor and respect men and women of God and to follow those as they follow Christ. These were often the spoken words across the pulpit to us as young adults, and as I grew older, these words and attributes remained a constant part of my daily commitment to my faith. I loved my pastor and first lady. They were the under-shepherds for my soul and my spiritual parents. They gave me the best advice concerning life, and I felt totally comfortable speaking with them pretty much about anything.

It was during my early twenties that things took a turn with the relationship between me and my first lady (my pastor's wife). I didn't quite understand it at first because I had allowed myself to follow a ritual, a teaching, a plan that made sense; however, I didn't study for myself the Word of God in its depth to find out how to honor and respect and to watch and pray diligently and consistently.

My first lady was gorgeous. She wore the best clothes, smelled of the most expensive perfumes, and nothing was ever out of place. She talked the talk and walked the walk. Her prayers were powerful, and everyone wanted to be just like her. But there was something hiding behind the "perfect figure" which was before us all. Our first lady lived a double life. She never spoke of it publicly because it would bring shame and reproach upon the church, but it wasn't until she and I started spending more time together on a one-on-one basis that I learned the truth and was led astray.

I was struggling with my flesh and trying to remain a virgin. Abstinence was the way of life for me until I married, but I was struggling within myself because I found myself seeing things on the television which would make my mind think about sex and being intimate with a man. My friends, most of whom were already sexually active, would talk about some of their experiences and how enjoyable it was and pleasurable. However, I still believed that God was able to keep me until the appropriate time—after I said, "I do" and was married, not before. So, I went to my first lady and spoke with her about my feelings and my struggles, and she gave me wise counsel each time on how to maintain myself without sinning.

However, one evening after she and I had met for dinner because I wanted to thank her for all of her help and support, things between us went sideways. As we were discussing our day, she placed her hand on top of mine and said she wanted to teach me another way of maintaining myself without having sex before marriage. I was totally open to the teaching—why not? This was my first lady. She would never lead me astray. So, she said we needed to go to my home and talk where it was more private.

As we arrived at my house, I was excited to find out how I could maintain my virginity and not compromise my faith by having sex before marriage. She and I sat on my couch, and I asked her what the secret or the trick was. She said, "There is no trick or secret. It is the only way to maintain before, during, and even after marriage."

The anticipation grew, and I said, "Come on, First Lady, stop holding back and teach me."

It was then she reached over and placed her hand in my vaginal area and said, "Masturbation. Allow me to help relieve you by stimulating your clit. This will give you an orgasmic release, and you will not need a man or sex. I can be the only one who will help you with this, and you don't have to tell anyone."

At this point, I was totally confused. Actually, I was ashamed because I wasn't sure if I wanted to try it or not. My friends spoke about self-pleasuring, but I was taught that it was sin, a form of perversion. Many of my Christian friends did not believe it was a sin to masturbate, but it definitely opens the door to allow for perverse thoughts and actions to occur.

But hold up, this was my first lady, my spiritual mother, and she was asking me to engage in lesbian acts. She wanted me to be her "lady," and she said it was all to help me not sin. When does a sin stop you from another sin? Then I remembered that Jesus told the Pharisees about casting out the devil, that "if Satan cast out Satan, he is then divided against himself; how shall then his kingdom stand" (Matthew 12:26)? No. This was a trick of the enemy, and my first lady was not a first lady at all—she was a perverse lady.

How did we even get to this point? Everyone struggles with something in their lifetime, but as leaders within the body of Christ, they ought to lead others to righteousness, not damnation. So, I got up and told my first lady that I was not interested in being her "first lady" and that it was time for her to go.

Sadly, every time I saw her after that experience, I saw the sadness behind her eyes and realized that a sex-starved husband or wife is just as dangerous as a sex-craved woman or man. No one is less or more prone to sexual sin—we all need help!

OVERCOMING:PHYSICAL RAPE

Rape or molestation, regardless of who commits it, is wrong. No one should be forced to have sexual encounters or engage in unwelcomed sexual acts or gestures with anyone forcibly or without prior permission. No means no, and yet there are many who have unfortunately dealt with physical rape and/or abuse within the religious communities and from members of the body of Christ.

If you are a victim, it is your duty and right to tell someone. It is your responsibility to free yourself by revealing it to someone you can trust in order to allow God to heal you from your spiritual and physical pains. You do not have to continue living daily with the quiet storm within your mind and heart, regardless of how people may look at you. Bringing awareness to the predators in effort to help someone else be free from this perverse and unclean demon is not only your duty but your right.

Rape is wrong, manipulation and molestation are wrong, abuse in any shape or form is wrong, and for anyone to exert their authority and power to force their way upon you is illegal, wrong, and, most importantly, not of God.

If you don't stand for something, you just might fall for anything. Silence is not always golden.

Being raped or abused, regardless of how, is traumatizing in and of itself. However, the physical abuse and anguish rendered upon those who unfortunately have experienced such horrible act(s) tend to have long lasting effects. Nevertheless, there is nothing wrong with speaking up. You have a voice and help is available.

Scripture teaches us, "You have not because you ask not. (James 4:2)" Sometimes we think no one cares or understands what we are going through, but many times, it is because no one knows. So, how can we help if we don't know what's wrong?

How can we pray for you if you don't identify the need? Finding help when you need it can be challenging, but it is critical in the process of healing.

As an overcomer of some of these unfortunate situations, I have a personal understanding of the feelings of shame, guilt, confusion, and, most importantly, weakness. As a believer in the Lord, I felt as if I should be stronger to just let it go and trust that God would handle it all. There is some truth to this—yes, God is able and will continue to handle it all—but God also wants us to pray for our enemies, seek wise counsel during times of complexities, and use our voices to help stop the spread of the sinful nature in the effort to help someone else.

I am a witness that you too can and will overcome. Daily prayer and seeking God for His direction are pivotal in moving forward. Find a support group or a person who you can trust to become your mentor or advocate to help you through your recovery. Be honest with yourself about how you feel, but don't get stuck at the crossroads of life and stay in the place of hurt. Take the hurt and pains and find out, through prayer and meditation of the Word of God, how to replace the pain with praise, how to move from madness to victory, and how to shine your light when the darkness has tried to overtake you. It is a moment-by-moment journey, yet you can overcome and be free from the traps that the enemy tries to set.

CHAPTER 3

EMOTIONAL RAPE

ONE DAY I'M UP, AND the next day, I'm down. It feels like I'm on an emotional rollercoaster. I'm not bipolar—I'm just human. Feelings of anxiety overcome me from time to time, yet the Word of God says, "Be anxious for nothing, but in everything by prayer and supplication, with thanksgiving, let your requests be made known to God; and the peace of God, which surpasses all understanding, will guard your hearts and minds through Christ Jesus. (Philippians 4:6-7)" But what in the world does that really mean when I am emotionally drained by the constant back and forth with church drama and inconsistencies with the leaders at my church?

I understand that there is great chaos and dysfunction in this world, but, Lord, please help me because sometimes I feel like there is more peace outside the church than inside. I am perplexed in my mind but not in despair. Sometimes I have thoughts which take over and cause me to wonder if I am really saved or set apart from the world. Then I go and ask for help yet find no answers.

Emotional abuse is sometimes greater to overcome than physical. The mind is a place where secrets lie, breakdowns occur, and anguish or torment is captured. Yet, there is still hope—or is there? Yes, there is. The hope of glory is a deliverer. The Word of God is greater and can captivate the thoughts which seem to overwhelm us. But why does it seem like the words spoken over my life are not active? Why do I feel like I am being emotionally manipulated by the ones I trust? Is it me? Do I have a magnet for people to come and abuse my love and my peace?

No, there is a bigger issue which comes to play in the minds of believers. The answer is "the will of God."What? The will of God? How does that play a part with emotional abuse or rape of my mind? Many people chase after immediate gratification or instant removal of negativity or problems instead of seeking to find out what the will of God is concerning their issues or problems and how to take the necessary steps to overcome. Instead, we internalize the problems. We overthink and cloud our brains full of negative thoughts and actions, which we take and try to handle in our own strength. But we must look inward, past the pain and past the circumstances, and totally rely on God's strength to help us understand the "why" and the "what," even when we don't know the "how."

Emotional abuse comes from a place of void. When people have a void in their lives, they find ways of filling it, regardless of who or how it may hurt others. The problem with emotional abuse within the body of Christ is that people fail to realize that God does not seek for us to move or act according to our emotions or how we feel. It is not a feeling but rather a knowing. What do you know about yourself? What do you know about God? What do you know about your life and your purpose? Many of us don't know anything about anything, so we play on the minds of others to persuade them to know what we want them to without seeking to find truth. No matter what people say or do, chase after wisdom to know what the good, acceptable, and perfect will of God is concerning you. That way, you can guard your heart with all diligence and not allow the words people speak and things people do cause you to become emotionally raped in your mind, which will then turn into a bitter root and, ultimately, a stronghold in your life.

Emotional Rape: Manipulation from the Pulpit

"We will be having evening service starting next week at 7:00 pm along with our normal 7:00 am and 11:00 am services. All leaders are required to be here, and if you are not here at all services, we will be taking attendance, and your titles will be revoked."

What? Another service? I am already away from home most of the day on Sundays with the two services. Then we attend Wednesday night Bible study, Friday night prayer service, and now, an added service. I am not sure how my husband will handle this one. He is very supportive and is active in ministry as well, but we have small children. We are unable to go to all of these services. But the pastor is requiring us to go; otherwise, our leadership and ministry positions may be taken away.

So, my husband and I go to talk with the pastor to find out if he really expects us to be at all of the services. As we sit with him, he expresses that it is the duty and responsibility of church leaders to attend all of the services, whether or not anyone else shows. "But how can we do all of this and still maintain a balance with our family life?" The pastor tells us to pray about it and make it work.

Later that evening, we receive a telephone call from one of the elders of the church. The elder further explains the need for us to be at church during the times that the pastor has indicated and that if we are unable to attend as requested, we need to let them know, and they will elect someone else to be put in our ministry positions.

This was a burden on us. We had been faithful to God through our actions to the ministry, but we also realized that our first ministry was to our family. For the order of God is personal relationship with God, family, and then church (others). Many times, people get it backwards and put the church before family, and this is where we find many issues.

So, on that following Sunday, my husband and I gave the elder a letter to give to the pastor (as this was the protocol at our church—you didn't just go up to the pastor and start talking. You had to schedule a meeting or give your information to one of the elders, and he would relay it to the pastor). Then, we requested to meet with the pastor during the week to discuss our letter with him.

Well, I guess he read the notice before he commenced preaching because when he got up to start, he stated that his sermon had been changed by the Holy Spirit. As he began to preach, he started speaking about lack of commitment and how people put everything and everyone before the work of the ministry and that that is out of order. *Out of order in whose book?* ran through my mind.

Then he continued to express how people said they loved him and cared about the ministry but neglected to follow through on what they said they would do to help the ministry grow. A warfare began in our hearts and our minds. As my husband and I both looked at each other, we felt the pull of anger festering up in both of us.

Then, it came full circle. The pastor started asking the congregation, "Who wants to be used by God? Who wants to do more in this ministry because we have available slots. God will only use those who avail themselves. If you are too busy for God and this ministry, then maybe God will be too busy for you when you need Him."

We couldn't believe it. How could our under-shepherd, our pastor, use these gimmicks and schemes from the pulpit to draw people in and put them in positions as a mechanism to get back at us for choosing to do what was right? It was manipulation and a power struggle coming from the headship/pulpit, which should never be. Emotional abuse and misuse of authority without seeking God for direction is a very dangerous place. This is misguided and misappropriation of authority and power upon the people. God help us all!

Emotional Rape: Gang Rape—"Clique Abuse"

"Yesssss, Pastor! You better preach it!"

"Come on now, Pastor. You are on it today!"

The voices echoed from the "Amen Corner," as we used to call them at church. These were the groups of people who would always yell and scream as the cheering section for the pastor (regardless if the message was good or bad or if we were at our home church or out visiting at another church. Some call them "cliques," and others call them "groupies." Nonetheless, these groups can be very toxic to the body of Christ if left unwatched and free to do whatever, whenever, and however they please).

Many wondered if they did this just for attention or if there was some underlying reason for the constant cheering squad because if others didn't join in, they were shunned, put down, and basically treated like outsiders, rather than part of the church body.

Well, one day, I brought my twelve-year-old granddaughter to church with me. It was a hot, summer afternoon, and we decided to go to the evening service because she had arrived at my home past the early morning service and it would get hot at church due to the large crowds.

During service, my granddaughter leaned over to me and asked why a group of ladies were wearing a similar style of clothing and if they were part of a special group. I explained to her that they were close friends and they oftentimes purchased fabric or special material and made their clothes to match. This was customary in African churches, but we were in a non-denominational, multi-ethnic church, so this group of ladies stood out from all the rest. I told her not to focus on them and their attire but to stay focused on the message from the pastor.

Then, the pastor got up to preach, and not even three good words into his sermon, one of the ladies in the group started edging him on, shouting with a loud voice, "Go 'head Pastor! You're surely preaching today."

I looked around to see if it was only me because he had just taken his text and hadn't gotten into his message yet. But I guess I was slow and missed something. Not even a few seconds later, another shouted out, and another, and another, and my granddaughter tapped my leg and asked, "Grandma, are we all supposed to do this when Pastor is preaching, or are we supposed to remain quiet and listen to his message?" I had to quickly explain that everyone responds to the Word of God differently but we all must do things decent and in order, not for show or attention. Soon, mostly everyone in the church was on their feet and shouting back at the pastor with words of encouragement and to tell him how great he was doing. But I was still sitting beside my granddaughter, trying to gain insight on the message that he was trying to preach. I had missed some of the points because of all of the shouting and yelling coming from his "fan club."

Now, let's get this clear. I am not casting stones at those who encourage our pastor. I think it is great. There are times when I even get up and clap and praise the pastor for the message which he is teaching or preaching, but not every Sunday. That's not me.

So, as we prepared to leave, a few of the ladies from the "Amen Corner" came over to speak to me and my granddaughter. And as soon as we finished speaking to one another and preceded to walk away, I overheard one of them say, "I don't know why she even comes here anyway; she never supports Pastor, and no one knows her really anyway." At this time, my granddaughter over-heard them and stopped and asked me what they meant. I asked her to wait for me at the door and that I would be right back. I then went to my so-called "sister-in-the-Lord" and asked her if there was an issue because the Word of God says that if you have an issue with your brother/sister, you should go to him/her. I didn't want to leave church with ill feelings due to a misunder-standing of what I thought I had overheard them say.

Sadly, the group of ladies (also known as a church "clique") together started pointing out ways in which I did not support the pastor and his ministry and explained that if I did not join in the ways they helped around the church, then I was a hindrance.

Wait...What? If I didn't "join" the ways in which "they" did things around the church, then I was a hindrance? Seriously? When did my support for the ministry become predicated upon following in the footsteps of those who group themselves together for the same cause or purpose? It's people like this (cliques within the church and the body of Christ) who sow dis-cord among the brethren, and God despise these types of people.

Doesn't the Word of God say we are individuals one of another and each have different functions yet one Lord, different ministries yet one body (1 Corinthians 12:4)? We are a body fitly joined together, but we all have individual goals and function-alities. Many people face these types of groups or cliques within the church often, but we must not be torn away or shifted from the focus on God's Word and His promises concerning our lives.

As I walked away, I started praying for them and for all of the other members within the church. But it was the Holy Spirit who stopped me and prompted me to pray for our pastor. It is him who needed to be covered by the blood of Jesus concerning such people. Clique abuse is real, and some may become very con-trolling and manipulative; however, God is bigger and stronger and is in full control!

Emotional Rape: The Guilt Trip

I can't believe what I am hearing. Is the pastor discussing the details of what I spoke to her in private just the other day in her sermon? Not again. This can't be happening to me right about now. It's bad enough that I am dealing with these issues at home, but now I have my business spread across the pulpit and the church. Everyone in church already knows that I am interested in becoming the new praise and worship leader, but by the time she finishes, everyone will probably figure out that it is me she is talking about. Well, maybe she isn't talking about me. Maybe there are others dealing with my same issue. Who knows? God does. I need to calm down and not judge the messenger and pay attention to the message, but why do I feel so betrayed, so degraded, so filthy as the pastor explains the sin that I already know rests upon me.

It was a few months ago, and I was going through a rough time at work and at home.Bills were due, and it seemed as though I just could not make ends meet. I prayed and prayed and prayed and asked God for direction, but it seemed as if God was nowhere to be found. I didn't hear anything. For days, I kept praying and asking God for some answers on what to do and how to make these ends meet. All I needed was a sign from God.

A couple days later, I received a call from a dear friend. To be more specific, this was a past lover. He was the one who I had called my "sure thing," my "true love," the one who I had said was my soulmate. But we were toxic. The only thing we had in common was our physical attraction for one another. But something about him kept me connected. It seemed as if every time I was in trouble or needed assistance (financially, emotionally, whatever), he would turn up and help. But his help came at a price.

So, I rejected his calls and didn't pay attention to the text messages coming through on my phone all times of the night. I just continued to tell myself, "I have been delivered from my past. Turning back means I am not fit for the kingdom. There is better for me, and God is my source." This helped for approximately three days; then I got the call from my children's school that I was behind on childcare payments and that unless I paid immediately, my children could not stay at before and aftercare. How could I work without having care for them before and after school? I was a single mom. I had been diligent all other times and had just hit a bad spot. I had been faithful to my commitment to fellowship at church and was striving to maintain so I could become the new praise and worship leader.

As I laid in my bed, perplexed in my mind, I figured one call wouldn't hurt. I could just tell him that I needed his help but without the "benefits" and that I would pay him back. Convinced within myself as to how it would play out, I called him. And as before, he came to my rescue. But this time, he said he didn't want the usual, which was normally a nightcap or to spend some private one-on-one time with me. No, this time, he wanted something more—he wanted a ménage à trois (a sexual encounter involving three people). This was an absolute no in my book. It was bad enough that I was preparing to sin by having sex with only him, but a threesome? No way. Now, the thoughts of what I was dealing with raced through my head. Do it or not? Childcare paid or possibly lose my job? God, where are You? I trust You, but I need You to help me. The time came for me to either "put up or shut up," so I gave in. A threesome happened, and guess what? I actually enjoyed it.

So, I went to my pastor to talk with her about this because I was now caught between a rock and a hard place. I had opened myself up to sin, and it had now taken me to a place that I never knew I would be in. I cried day and night asking God to forgive me, and I knew that I needed wise counsel because my mind would race with guilt and shame but then I would be reminded of the pleasure side of it.

As the pastor and I talked, she took me to scriptures about forgiveness, choices, sexual immorality, faith, and waiting on God. It was a good discussion, I thought. We ended it with prayer, and she ensured me that our conversation was private. Or was it really?

So, why was the pastor speaking about it now across the pulpit?—telling others that the wages of sin are death and that you can't be the praise and worship leader of this church if you are having sex out of wedlock and practicing sexual immorality. Was it me, or did it feel like every time I went to speak with the pastor, my information became a sermon topic? I was trying not to feel angry at her because what was being said was critical for the growth of the church, but wasn't there a way to get the point across without exposing someone's dirty laundry?

Then, the pastor pointed to many in the congregation and said, "And if any of you associate with people who are living double lives or living in sin, you are just as guilty, and the penalty is greater for you." I felt so guilty then—the shame of what I had done and the guilt of actually telling the pastor about it. Hold up—shouldn't my guilt be of the sin which I committed and not of the actions by the pastor? I kept checking myself because I had misplaced anger, and now, I had gone from one extreme to the other. I felt raped in my mind. My emotions were being pulled in many different directions, and I just wanted the anguish and torment to stop.

OVERCOMING:EMOTIONAL RAPE

"You shall not surley die" (Genesis 3:1-5) as Satan twisted the words and instructions spoken by God to Adam and Eve in the

Garden of Eden in effort to manipulate and cause them to sin. And now more than 2,000 years later, Satan still says these same words to each of us to cause us to doubt and ultimately disobey what God has said to us concerning our lives and our destiny.

Emotional abuse or mental rape are direct encounters with the enemy himself. It is his way of perverting words and changing them up to confuse the minds of believers in order to cause them to turn away from the truth, turn away from the faith, and, ultimately, turn away from God. But the devil knows that we win. He understands that by and through the Word of God, all things are established and made right. It is the Word of God that counteracts the intent and ways of the devil. How? The Word of God shines light on those dark areas of our lives. It shows us where the darkness of sin through our thoughts and deeds are, and it helps us move or flee away from those very appearances and turn to the light of God's love and live our lives in total victory.

Just as Satan tried to tempt Jesus and tried to mix up God's words, Jesus knew what was said by Abba Father and Jesus did not stray away from the truth and promises of God, which are yes and amen (2 Corinthians 1:20). The same stands true for you today. Satan uses the Word of God and tries to manipulate or distort the words being said or taught in an effort to bring you to a confused, compromised, or complacent place, which will lead to sin and destruction (and finally, spiritual death).

Many of the actions by people within the body of Christ can cause others pain, feelings of abuse, and misguided thoughts. But we must remember that the Lord says that our thoughts are not His thoughts and our ways are not His ways. His thoughts and ways are higher than our own. For there is a way that seems right unto man, but the end is destruction and death (Isaiah 55:8-9). We must seek to know the will and the way of the Lord and not seek after having our feelings and emotions tickled by those in authority. The time has come where people will have itching ears, looking to be seduced by words which make them feel good (emotionally) but not be satisfied by the truth of God's Word, which has come to change lives and to bring hope.

These different occurrences are not shown to cast a shadow upon the body of Christ; however, they bring light to dark areas which we tend to look past and not address. Many leaders don't realize some of the emotional damage which is happening within their congregations or from them personally. No one is exempt from being hurt or hurting others by words spoken or actions done. But we are commissioned to guard one another's reputations. We are to help bridge gaps between our sisters and brothers and not be the one pulling them apart or causing discord among the brethren. There comes a time within our spiritual journey that we take inventory of our actions and realize that our personal emotional baggage is just as heavy as rendering emotional weights on others.

So, how do we overcome emotional abuse or rape?:

As you may know, first, <u>pray</u>. Why? Prayer will be the key to unlock the mysteries concerning your life. It is communication between you and God, and you need direction and also correction as to what you have experienced and how to respond. Moreover, you must do as Jesus did. He prayed before going into the wilderness. We all will have a wilderness experience, a time full of things going "wild." But you don't have to stay there. Just as Jesus, our Savior and Lord, taught us, you can and will overcome by first understanding what God's plan for your life is and what He wants out of you.

Secondly, <u>study the Word of God</u>. You need to study to show yourself approved. You are a workman who needs not to be ashamed but to rightly divide the Word of Truth (2 Timothy 2:15). The issue that we face is that people will say things to and about us, and if we do not know our own truth, we can easily fall into the traps and believe what has or will be said. What does

God say about you? You are more than a conqueror. You are the head and not the tail. You are above and not beneath. You are a lender and not a borrower. You are loved, and you are the apple of God's eyes. You are His sheep and the sheep of His pasture.

There are many things concerning your life that God has spoken, but do you know what He has said about your life? It is difficult to overcome evil with good if you don't know the good that is within you. So, study the Word of God. Know what God says about you, and be ready to tell the devil through the Word of God that he is a liar and a defeated foe—why, because you know the truth about God concerning you.

And then, lastly, <u>renew your mind</u>. Fill your mind with things that are good and pleasant and will encourage you. The old saying, "An empty or idle mind is the devil's workshop," has some validity. Our emotions stem from our mental thoughts. We have to renew our minds daily and think on things which will help rejuvenate our minds to become better, wiser, and stronger. Every time your mind causes you to think negatively, counteract it with something that is good. No, it will not always be this easy, but you are capable to do this because God has given us the free will to choose. So, choose this day—peace over pressure, joy over sadness, emotional stability over emotional torment. I urge you to choose life, choose peace, and choose liberty and the pursuit of happiness.

Regardless of what people may think about you or say, have a strong sense of knowing who you are in Christ Jesus and take the steps to move forward in your newfound freedom.

THE REVEALED TRUTH ... "LET THE HEALING BEGIN"

T HERE IS NOTHING NEW UNDER *the sun. Since the days* of Adam and Eve, sin has been rampant and has shown its ugly face in the form of despair, manipulation, abuse, rape, greed, pride, and many other forms in effort to distract, distort, kill, steal, and destroy the work of the cross of Jesus Christ and dismantle the functionality and power of the body of Christ.

Although many of these situations have caused a great separation within the body of Christ, we have to reflect on what is the purpose and the plan for these occurrences. God never intended for His people to hurt. He never intended for His people to be abused. Nor did God plan for His people to be pulled away by the careless acts of others.

The "unveiling truth" is this—it is not the church that rapes. It's sin. Sin comes and knocks at the doorways of the hearts of us all, and it is our job to "flee from the very appearance of evil (sin) (1 Thessalonians 5:22)" and to cling or hold onto that which is right(eous) and good. The problem that we face, time and time again, is that the flesh is weak, and many fall prey to selfish acts of wrongdoings and neglect the denying of oneself in order to bring glory to God.

So, where does this leave us? All that has been written in this book is not to bring despair, reproach, negativity, or a cloud of darkness over the church but to bring the truth and an area of forgiveness, restoration, and hope to all who have been victimized or turned from that which we believe. Many people have shamed or doomed the body of Christ because of individuals who chose to yield (act on) the temptations of sin. Their actions resulted in terrible situations and hurt many people; yet, the church isn't to blame, but we do have a responsibility to help shield and protect one another. And for this, we as the church apologize for our mishandling of your soul and for the carelessness of allowing people and things to happen to tender hearts such as yours.

Life has a way of bringing many together, and in a split second, it also has a way of pulling nations apart. Sin is not to be tampered with; nor is it to be brushed under a rug and forgotten as if it never occurred. No, there is a repercussion for sin—a penalty for wrongdoings, a result for inflicting bad, hurt, and pain on others. But God is the final judge. Jesus paid the price of redemption for all of us. So, what is our job or responsibility?

First, we must pray—pray for ourselves and pray for our enemies. Why? Because prayer releases the problems, the situations, and the circumstances from our personal hands and transfers them to the Almighty One who is able to keep us all from falling. Prayer allows us a direct communication with the One who sees and knows all as we then give the power back to Him in order to move forward toward being whole.

Sin breaks, tears, and ultimately destroys. It causes a wedge between us and God. Not only that we personally have sinned, but we have also been sinned against; yet when we hold onto the hurt, pain, and wrongdoings and allow for the devil (Satan) to torment us in our minds, we then give way to allow sin to go rampant inside of us. The Word of God says, "Let this mind by in you which was also in Christ Jesus. (Philippians 2:5)" Jesus was wronged, He was beaten, He was talked about, people tried to manipulate Him, and those who carried titles tried to exert their authority over Him, but at the end, Jesus forgave.

So, secondly, we must forgive—forgive our enemies and for-give ourselves. Today, is your day to forgive yourself for allowing the pains to overtake you and for allowing the guilt of your past to dictate how you ought to live. Shame was never your por-tion. It was never destined for you. Today is your day to lift up your head and open your heart to a clean and right start in Jesus Christ and to reflect on the good. For we ought to "think on those things that are pleasant, righteous, and of a good report. (Philippians 4:8)" But you say, how do I do that? The answer—by renewing your mind,

Next, you have to fill your thoughts with things which will bring peace, joy, encouragement, and hope. It is not easy, but you can do it. You are more than an overcomer. So, to overcome, you must **come over** the situation. You must move forward and not be afraid to face the truth that you are not alone and you are not going to stay in that space of hopelessness.

Lastly, for you who have been struggling in this area(s), for all who have questioned where to go and who to turn to, and for all who have decided not to attend a fellowship or go to "church buildings" anymore because of what has been said or done to you or how you may feel, today is your day of restoration. Today is your day for salvation. Today is your day for newness of life through Jesus Christ. You may be that person who started out in the faith and turned because of some or one of these circum-stances. Come back! You may have decided that you don't need to be among other people to believe in God, and you are correct, but the Word of God clearly tells us, "Don't forsake the assem-bling of yourselves.(Hebrews 10:25)" Why is that? Because I need you, and you need me. It is not a cliché. It is truth. When we come together, we ignite hope, love, and a passion for God together.

**For we are the church, not the building. Regardless of where we assemble, we are the church.**

So, no, you were not raped by the church. Sin within someone caused this, and now it's time to get your life back. Blaming the church or even God isn't the correct answer.

You may feel justified to blame someone or something, but when you rightly divide that which is true versus that which is false, you find out that the church buildings or gatherings of the saints are not gatherings of perfect people but people in need of a Savior, people in need of continued strength, and people who are daily fighting temptations from the enemy.

Now, stand up and be strong in the Lord and in the power of His might. Put your armor of the Word of God back on, and let's battle in the Spirit. For "we wrestle not against flesh and blood but against principalities, powers of the darkness, evil that destroys. (Ephesians 6:12)"

But some may say, "I am not the one who was affected by any of these acts. I am just reading this book, and I don't know where or how this applies to me." Well, this applies to you because nothing happens by mistake. You are to share this good news with others because you just may be the vehicle, the Word of Truth, the Bible, the Good News, that people will see. Encourage someone today and realize that it was God who held back some or even all of these situations from you. Hallelujah!

Not all are evil. Not all are good. But one thing remains certain and true—God loves you, and He remains faithful, even when we are not faithful to Him. Jesus died on the cross for everyone, so accept the sacrifice of His blood and return to Him today. "For all have sinned and come short of the Glory of God! (Romans 3:23)" **_Salvation, restoration, healing, and God's love are for all!_**

****

If you are unfortunately a victim of abuse within the body of Christ, say this prayer (out loud) with me as I stand in agreement with you for your restoration, salvation, repentance, hope, and love:

Dear God,

Thank you for loving me. Thank you for keeping me. Thank you for allowing me this opportunity to come back to You. It has not been easy. My life has been a whirlwind of ups and downs. But God, I know now that with You, all things will work together for my good. Even when it seems like my life is in full chaos, You are still working it out for my good. So, I repent for not fully trusting You. I repent for not fully surrendering to You. I repent for not releasing all this pain and hurt to You. I wanted others to feel my pain. I wanted others to feel my hurt. But it was all paid on the cross when Jesus, Your only begotten Son, took on my pain, hurt, doubts, and fears, and I thank you, Jesus, for dying for me. Now, God, I open my heart to You without holding anything back. I accept You into my life to be my God and my King. I accept Jesus Christ as my Lord and my Savior. And I accept the free gift of the Holy Spirit to teach me and comfort me during the rest of my life. When my eyes fill with tears, read them. As my heart starts to change from a stony heart to a heart of flesh, please cover me. As I place my entire being into Your hands, please allow the Holy Spirit to lead and guide me into all truth as I continue upward in my newness of life. Now, Father God, I pray for all who have wronged me, and I ask You to forgive me for all of the wrong I have done to others. I pray for all of the leaders who have mishandled Your sheep and Your resources, and I pray that You will bring us all into oneness and unity by and through Your love. I know now I am restored back into the fold. I know now I am redeemed and forgiven. I know now that I am able to live my life no longer bound by what has happened or what the enemy may try to throw my way. I love you, Father God, and I accept my new life of freedom, which is only found in You. Now I seal this prayer with the blood of Jesus Christ. Amen.

Hallelujah! Glory to God! Welcome back. You are saved, and you are restored. It may not feel different, but you are different. Life may not look different, but it is different. Now, live your best life. For your "later days shall be far greater than your former, (Haggai 2:9)" so possess it and go!

※※※※※※※※

If you are unfortunately an abuser upon the body of Christ (a leader or person who has misused your title or authority or exerted your ways on others under the guise of religion or Christianity), and you want to truly be free from your past and turn from your wicked ways, say (out loud) this prayer with me as I stand in agreement with you for full restoration, salvation, forgiveness, and love:

Heavenly Father,

I acknowledge that You are my Savior and You are my Lord. I recognize that I have sinned and have come short of Your glory. I recognize and acknowledge that I have hurt others and have misused Your love and Your trust as I have tried things my way and have yielded to temptations, which have resulted in abuse, pain, and overall sin. Father God, I need You. I cannot make another step without You. I thank you that You have not allowed me to die in my sin; yet You have given me this opportunity to come to You right now to correct my wrongs and to repent and turn from my wicked ways. Heavenly Father, You see all and know all, and I have tried to cover up ways which are not pleasing to You, and I ask for Your forgiveness. I know that I must make right and correct the errors of my ways, but first, I must come to You because I am unable to face those who I have wronged, and the feelings of guilt and shame are forever upon me. I open my heart to You and ask that You forgive me for guiding Your people to dark places. Forgive me for perverting Your gospel and rendering it upon those who You have placed in my trust. I know Your heart breaks when I choose my way, but now, I turn fully from my personal agendas, and I totally yield to Your will and way for my life. Give me the strength to stand firm on Your Word and to apply it to my life first before sharing it with others. I now pray for everyone who I have allowed to hurt me. For I know that hurting people hurt people. The curse of pain stops here and now. The curse of rejection and perversion stops here and now. The curse of despair and manipulation stops here and now. The curse of allowing people to run and rule over me stops here and now. I choose peace. I choose joy. I choose obedience. I choose uprightness. I choose to trust in You and You alone. I choose love and restoration upon my life so that I am able to give it according to Your Word and not according to my flesh. Thank you, Father God, for supplying all of my needs. Times are hard and tough, but You promised to give me what I need when I put my trust in You. Forgive me for being a hypocrite and standing before Your people with dirty hands and a dirty heart. I know now that as I have spoken, that shall it be. For out of the abundance of the heart, the mouth speaks. And from the heart flows the issues of life. My heart now beats completely for You. Help me through this journey called life that I may bring You glory and honor. Cover me and my family with the blood of Jesus that no hurt, harm, or danger may come to my dwelling. Thank you for restoring joy, salvation, and deliverance upon me. And now, lead and guide me through the Holy Spirit to reveal to heal that which will edify the body and not hurt it any longer. I receive Your love, rejuvenation, forgiveness, and truth right now, in Jesus's name. Amen!

Hallelujah! My fellow co-laborer in the Lord—I know this can be challenging, but I also know that God is able to see you through it all. If you believe this in your heart and confessed this with your mouth, you are saved, restored, and back in right standing with the Lord. Remember—to whom much is given, much is required. As a leader, God expects us to lead the people unto righteousness, so now take the step(s) and make right your wrongs and let full healing and restoration flow from you onto your congregation, your sheep, your family, those you have hurt, and those who have fallen away from the faith due to your negligence. God loves you, and many may not understand the pressure which comes from being ministry/spiritual leaders; yet all of us have to remember that we are all "fellows in the ship" (fellowship—of believers), and we all need the Lord.

Remember, it's not how you start but how you finish that makes the difference!

If you said either or both of these prayers and believe it in your heart, please write telling me how this has helped or encouraged you to: Joy in Jesus Ministries, P.O. Box 1124, Rancho Cucamonga, CA 91729, or visit www.joy-ministries.info.

MESSAGE FROM THE AUTHOR

HEAL:to mend, cure, make whole; return to original state of health

Are any among you in trouble? They should pray. Are any among you happy? They should sing praises. Are any among you sick? They should send for the church Elders, who will pray for them and rub olive oil on them in the name of the Lord. This prayer made in faith will heal the sick; the Lord will restore them to health, and the sins they have committed will be forgiven. So then, confess your sins to one another and pray for one another, so that you will be healed. The prayer of a good person has a powerful effect. (James 5:13-17)

****

Life has a way of bringing people together and also tearing them apart. I pray this book brings us all to a place of peace, joy, unity, and, most importantly, healing and restoration. I believe God has allowed for each of us to go through this journey called life to gain knowledge and wisdom in order to help one another.

As an overcomer of some of these experiences personally, I have a strong sense of knowing and have come to a place in my own life to realize and admit that I am not always right nor do I understand everything; but God, who knows and has everything and is always right, will allow for all things to work together for my good. Furthermore, I have learned over time that when I reveal my downs as well as my ups, many people can gain healing and love through the testimonies of my struggles, as well as from my successes.

As a mother of five beautiful children (Marquis, Koya, Marlin Jr., Mikkel, and Addison), I have come to an awareness that my responsibility is not only to protect, nurture, provide, and guide them but to also teach them the truth about the Word of God, the people of God, and also how the enemy (Satan) uses people inside and outside the body of Christ or religious settings to distort the truth about God and try to cause people to turn away from living victoriously through Jesus Christ and by the aid of the Holy Spirit. It is also my responsibility to reveal how sin (which also comes as a result of perverse and rebellious actions) hurts and abuses people in effort to kill, steal, and destroy. Yet, as overcomers, we can live our lives without compromising our faith in the Lord Jesus Christ and be free from the guilt and shame of our past.

As an ordained pastor, evangelist, and teacher, I have counseled and encouraged many people for many years, and I am no longer surprised at the various struggles people hide and/or disregard because of the potential backlash, incorrect rebukes, and shame which comes from revealing ill-mannered behaviors and perverse actions which should not be named among those who are believers in the Lord and Savior Jesus Christ.

So, I pray this book brings awareness to issues within the body of Christ and will prompt many not to fall prey to the various schemes and traps set by the enemy, which can result in abuse (physical, emotional, and financial). Furthermore, I pray that all who may have been victimized or abused by those who classify themselves as Christians or members of the body of the Christ and have strayed from the church because of such actions be reconciled back to the fold, healed within their hearts, and come to a place of forgiveness and strength in order to move forward and be set free and made whole.And most importantly, I hope this book allows all to know that they are not alone in this fight of faith and that with God, they can and will overcome.

Lastly, I desire that everyone who reads this book comes to the understanding that, "All have sinned and come short of the Glory of God" (Rom. 3:23) for we all need the Lord in our daily lives. Many spiritual leaders, pastors, preachers, bishops, etc. have failed in regards to fully protecting the "sheep," and for this reason, we uncover and expose some of the various traps and tactics of the enemy in order to correct, cleanse, make aware, and apologize to those who have been targeted and hurt by the lack of proper protection and guidance by our leaders. We further believe that through this book, reconciliation and restoration will take place within each of you. For God loves you, and there is nothing or no one who can ever take that love away from you.

I want to thank my husband, Lloyd G. Murphy, III, for his love, encouragement, support, prayers, and, most importantly, his covering for me and our family. To my sister, Koya M. Staten-Bakare, for her everlasting love and truth and for wiping my tears and praying for me when I didn't know how to pray for myself or who else to turn to. To Marlin Mims, who walked through the journey early on with me and never allowed me to give up on God when I felt God had given up on me. And to my mother (Patricia Staten), late grandmother (Mary V. Hart), late pastor (Bishop Philip C. Johnson), cousin (Janice Sims), aunt (Jeanette Smith), friends (Lakisha Wright, Debbie "Jazzy" Grant, and Deidra Bynum), and our faithful deacon (Tyrone Green), for your unwavering faith and prayers. And finally, to all who allowed me to include their story(ies) in this book in order to bring forth awareness that we may not walk or live in ignorance so that God may be glorified, the devil horrified, and the people edified to become better, healthier, and more whole as they overcome what many describe as "church rape."

You are loved, and God Bless.

"Deliverance can be instant, but the battle can be a lifetime. Yet you can overcome!"

Quote by Pastor Tahira Staten-Murphy

GLOSSARY

Rape: unlawful sexual activity and usually sexual intercourse carried out forcibly or under threat of injury against the will, usually of a female or with a person who is beneath a certain age or incapable of valid consent

Sex or Sexual Intercourse: sexual contact between individuals involving penetration, especially the insertion of a man's erect penis into a woman's vagina, typically culminating in orgasm and the ejaculation of semen.

Molestation: sexual assault or abuse of a person; the action of pestering or harassing someone in an aggressive or persistent manner.

Manipulation: control or influence (of a person or situation) that is clever, unfair, or unscrupulous; alteration of (data) or presentation of (statistics) so as to mislead.

Perversion: the alteration of something from its original course, meaning, or state to a distortion or corruption of what was first intended; sexual behavior or desire that is considered abnormal or unacceptable.

Clique: a narrow exclusive circle or group of persons, especially one held together by common interests, views; an exclusive group of associates that rarely allows others to join.

Abuse: use (something) to bad effect or for a bad purpose; misuse; treat (a person or an animal) with cruelty or violence, especially regularly or repeatedly; assault someone sexually; use or treat in such a way as to cause damage or harm; speak in an insulting and offensive way to or about (someone); the improper use of something; unjust or corrupt practice.

Church: public worship of God or a religious service in such a building; the whole body of Christian believers; Christendom, a body of Christians worshipping in a particular building or con-stituting one congregation.

CPSIA information can be obtained
at www.ICGtesting.com
Printed in the USA
BVHW081145220620
582039BV00002BA/223

9 781631 294235